First
1000 WORDS

JULIE HAYDON

HB

Hinkler BOOKS

First published in 2004
by Hinkler Books Pty Ltd
17-23 Redwood Drive
Dingley VIC 3172 Australia
www.hinklerbooks.com

© Hinkler Books Pty Ltd 2004

ISBN 1 7412 1402 5

Designer: Ivan Finnegan
Photography: Peter Wakeman
Printed & bound in China

CONTENTS

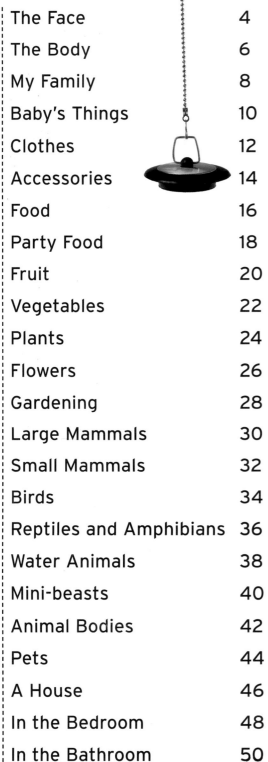

THE
Face

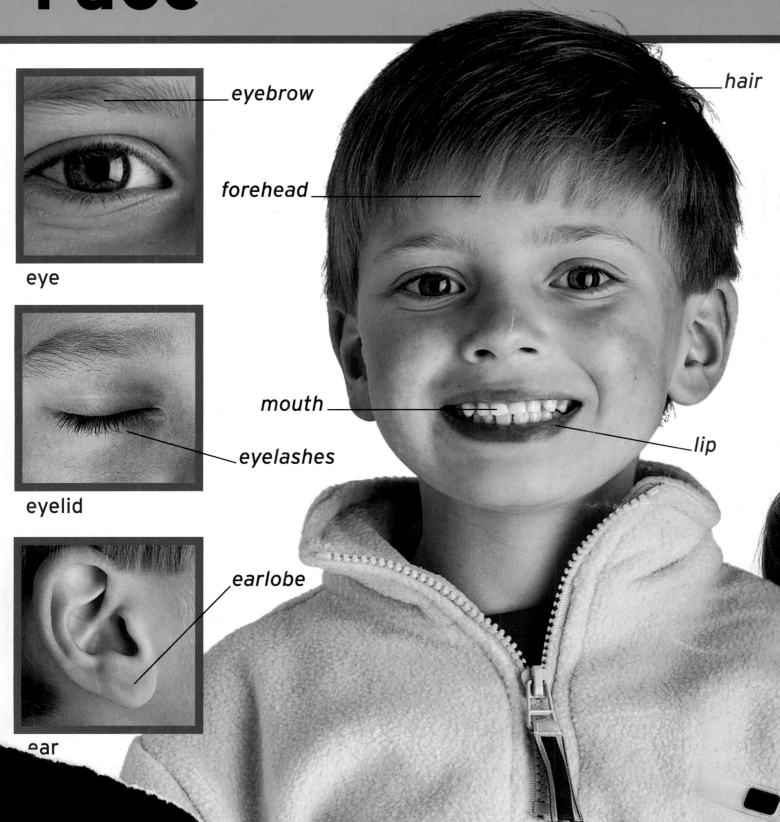

eyebrow

hair

eye

forehead

eyelashes

eyelid

mouth

lip

earlobe

ear

A HAPPY FACE

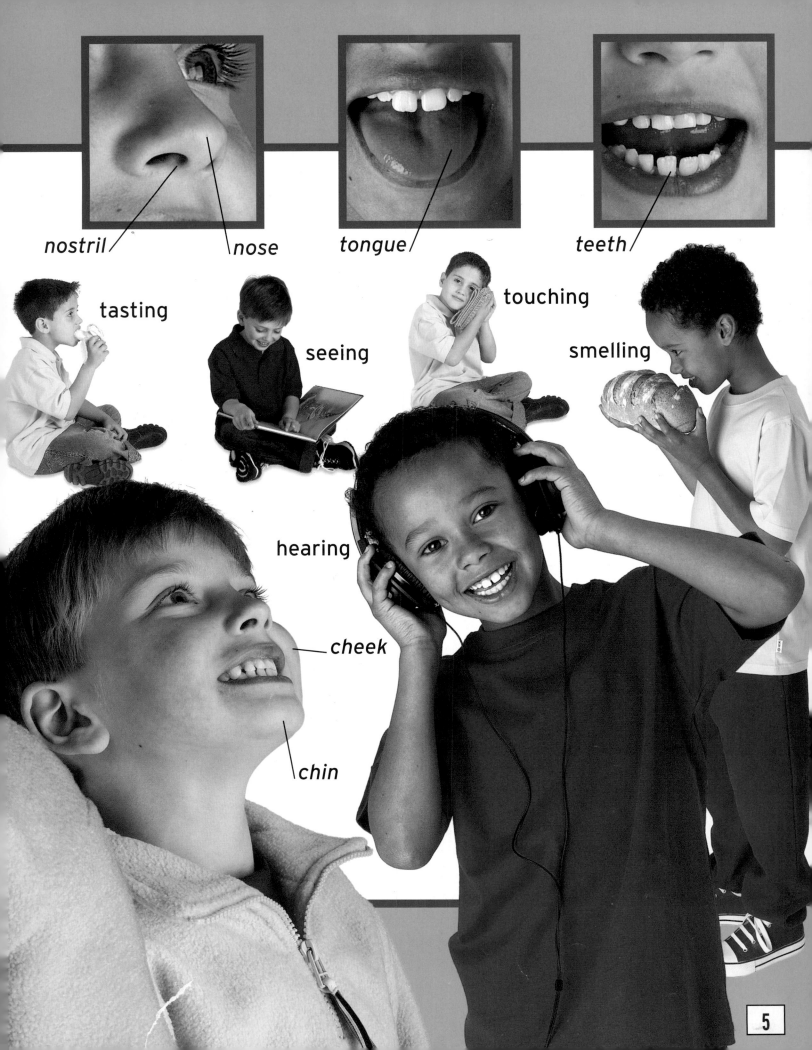

nostril *nose* tongue teeth

tasting

touching

seeing

smelling

hearing

cheek

chin

5

THE
Body

head

shoulder

neck

arm

chest

abdomen

finger

wrist

waist

hip

hand

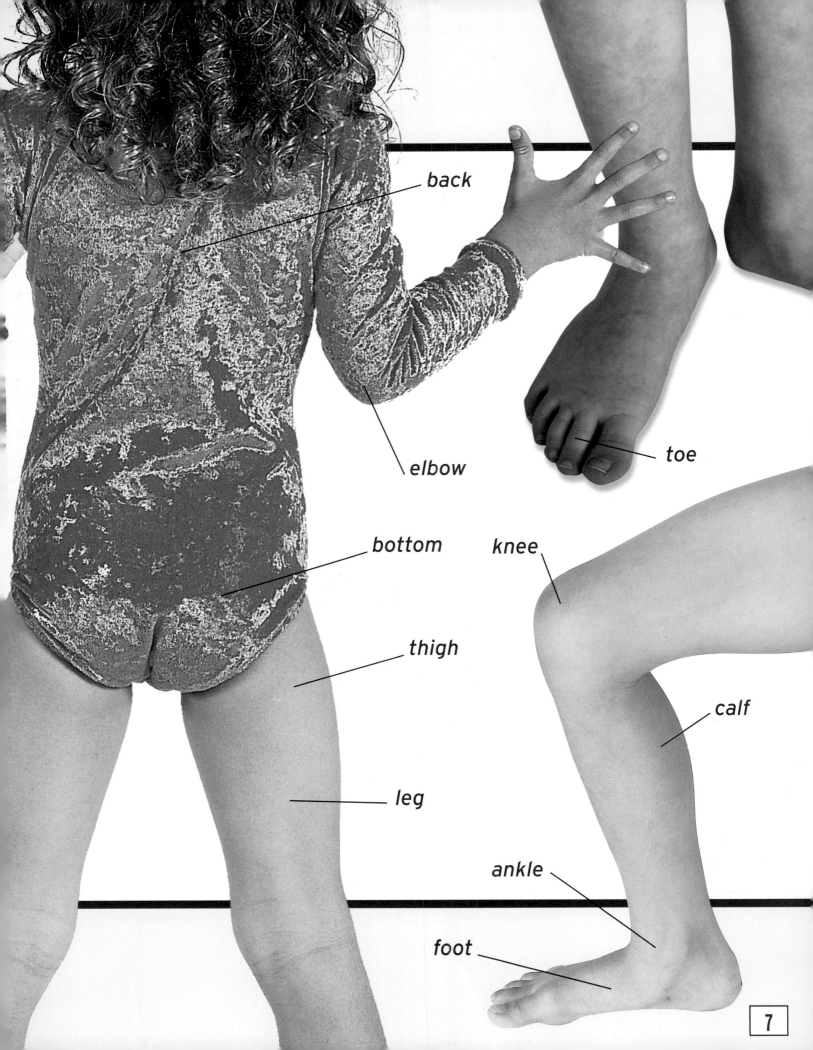

back

elbow

toe

bottom

knee

thigh

calf

leg

ankle

foot

MY Family

my birth certificate

my brother

my pa

my kitten

my nana

my twin

ME

BABY CHILD TEENAGER ADULT MY SURNAME

Simpson.

my uncle

my aunt

my photo album

my cousin

my father

my grandmother

my grandfather

my mother

my sister

9

BABY'S Things

bootees

blanket

pins

high chair

rattle

cotton balls

soft toy

powder

monitors

BIB

bottle

pacifier

jumpsuit

potty

diaper

mobile

wipes

stroller

cot

car seat

11

Clothes

tights

overalls

shorts

sweater

jeans

singlet

BOOTS

tie

underpants

coat

trousers

shoes

12

leotard

shirt

dress

T-shirt

skirt

socks

underpants

jacket

sneakers

13

Accessories

satchel

hat

hairclip

key ring

beret

EARRING

braces

headband

ribbons

necklace

scrunchies

backpack

handbag

evening bag

gloves

belt

watch

cap

rings

fake tattoo

bracelets

15

Food

egg

sandwich

sugar

butter

cereal

juice

yogurt

FISH

granola bars

bread

crackers

hot chocolate

16

oatmeal

milk

cheese

meat

rice

pasta

honey

salad

PARTY Food

muffin

fried chicken

potato chips

fruit tart

pies

JELLYBEANS

lollipop

donut

popcorn

jello

cookies

marshmallows

candy
cane

nuts

cake

chocolate

soda

pizza

hamburger

fries

19

Fruit

raspberry

cherries

kiwi fruit

tomato

avocado

grapefruit

ORANGES

pear

banana

olives

apricot

mangoes

mandarin
orange

strawberry

dates

pineapple

apple

lemon

watermelon

grapes

peaches

21

Vegetables

asparagus

onion

cabbages

leeks

carrots

SWEET CORN

cauliflower

radish

spinach

mushrooms

rhubarb

broccoli

zucchini

parsnip

beet

lettuce

green onions

turnip

potatoes

eggplant

peas

Plants

acorns

fern

grass

holly

ivy

cactus

blossom

LEAVES

seedling

pine cone

24

moss

trunk

bark

bottlebrush

wattle

gum flowers

palm tree

weeping willow

maple

oak leaves

flytrap

pot plants

25

Flowers

pansy

violet

bouquet

daisy

chrysanthemum

orchid

bluebell

SUNFLOWER

tulip

cornflower

knotweed

gardenia

zinnia

carnation

hibiscus

marigold

iris

rose

lily

freesia

gerbera

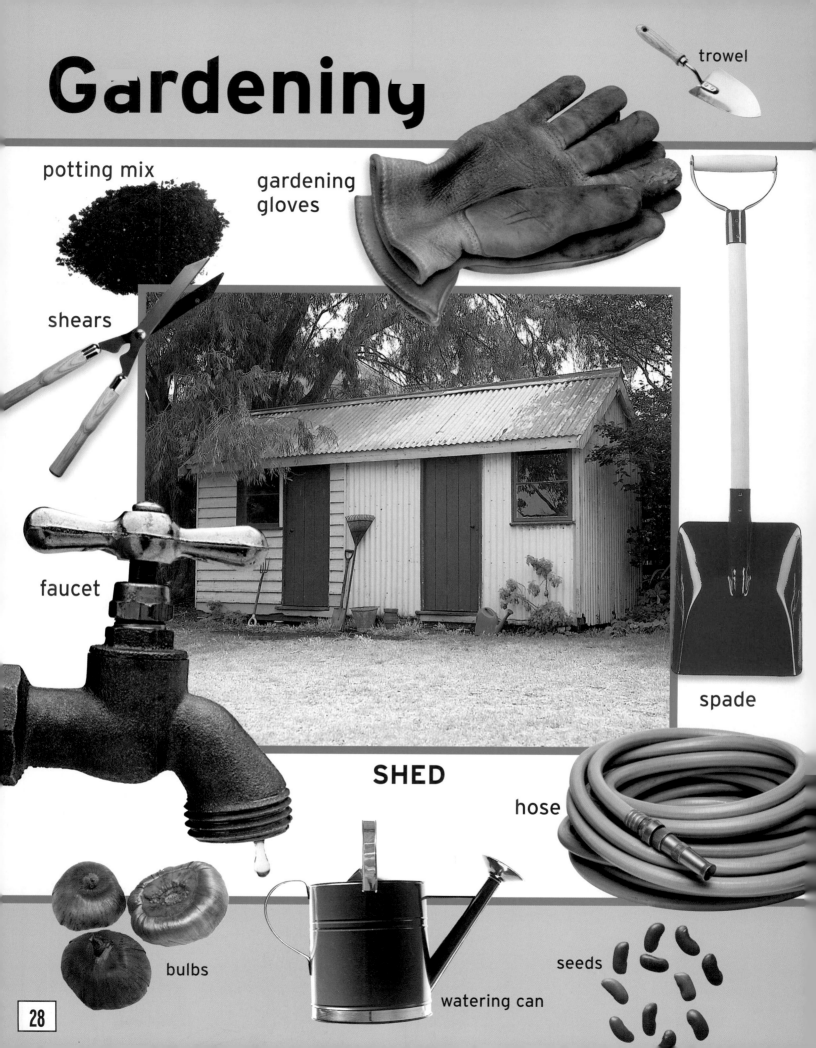

Gardening

trowel

potting mix

gardening gloves

shears

faucet

SHED

spade

hose

bulbs

watering can

seeds

compost bin

flowerpots

clippers

gardening hat

wheelbarrow

lawnmower

rake

shovel

weeds

rock

29

LARGE
Mammals

cheetah

tiger

lion

elephant

bear

WHALE

hippopotamus

seal

rhinoceros

polar bear

deer

monkey

dolphins

kangaroo

camel

leopard

giraffe

chimpanzee

puma

gorilla

moose

Birds

emu

pigeon

owl

kingfisher

puffin

parrot

ALBATROSS

eagle

macaw

pelican

ostrich

falcon

34

hawk

lovebird

flamingo

crane

peacock

toucan

swans

vulture

woodpecker

WATER Animals

puffer fish

lobster

herrings

tuna

oysters

prawn

angelfish

JELLYFISH

stingray

seadragon

coral

shark

damsel fish

cod

sardines

salmon

sea horse

starfish

catfish

crab

eel

pike

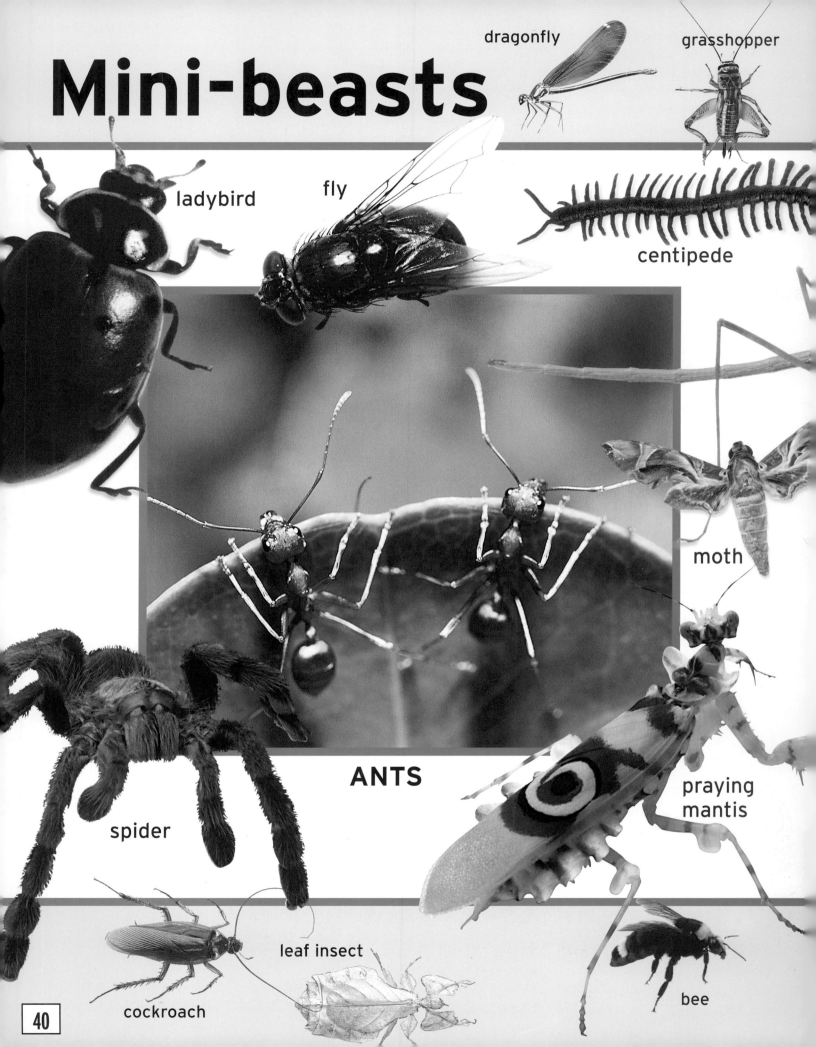

Mini-beasts

dragonfly

grasshopper

ladybird

fly

centipede

moth

ANTS

spider

praying
mantis

leaf insect

cockroach

bee

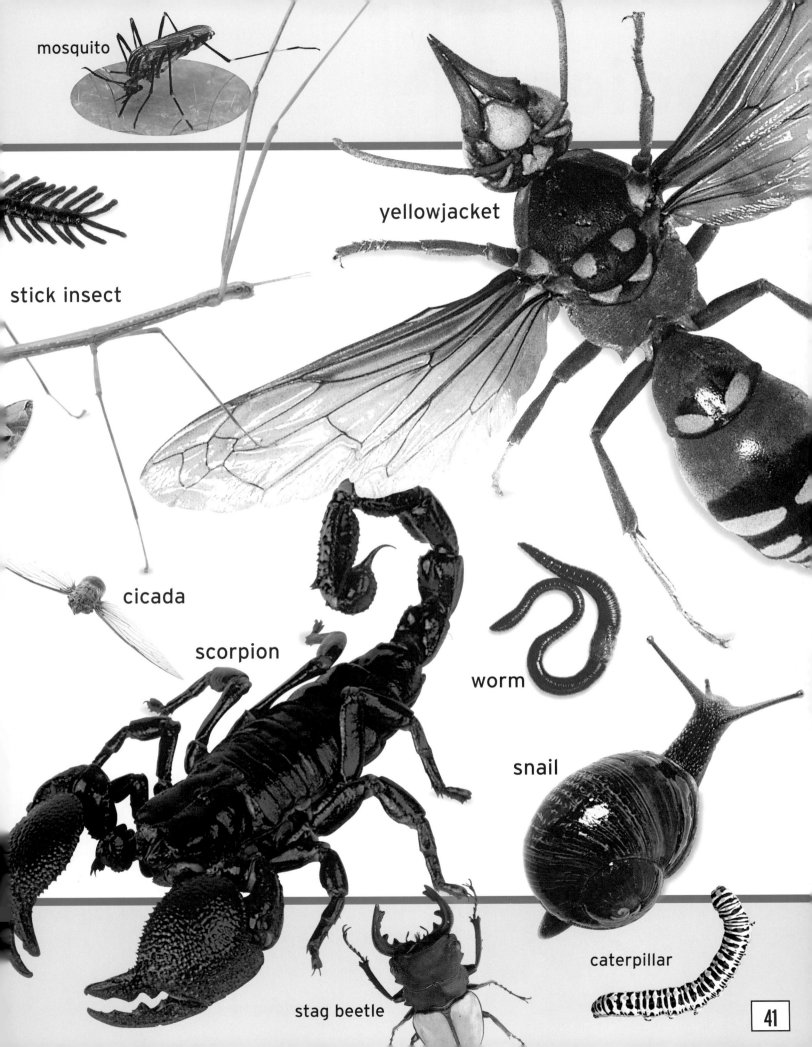

mosquito

yellowjacket

stick insect

cicada

scorpion

worm

snail

stag beetle

caterpillar

ANIMAL
Bodies

hoof

feathers

horn

wings

FANGS

fur

tail

spines

alons

whiskers

42

scales

paw

claws

gill

mane

snout

antlers

pouch

tusks

fin

beak

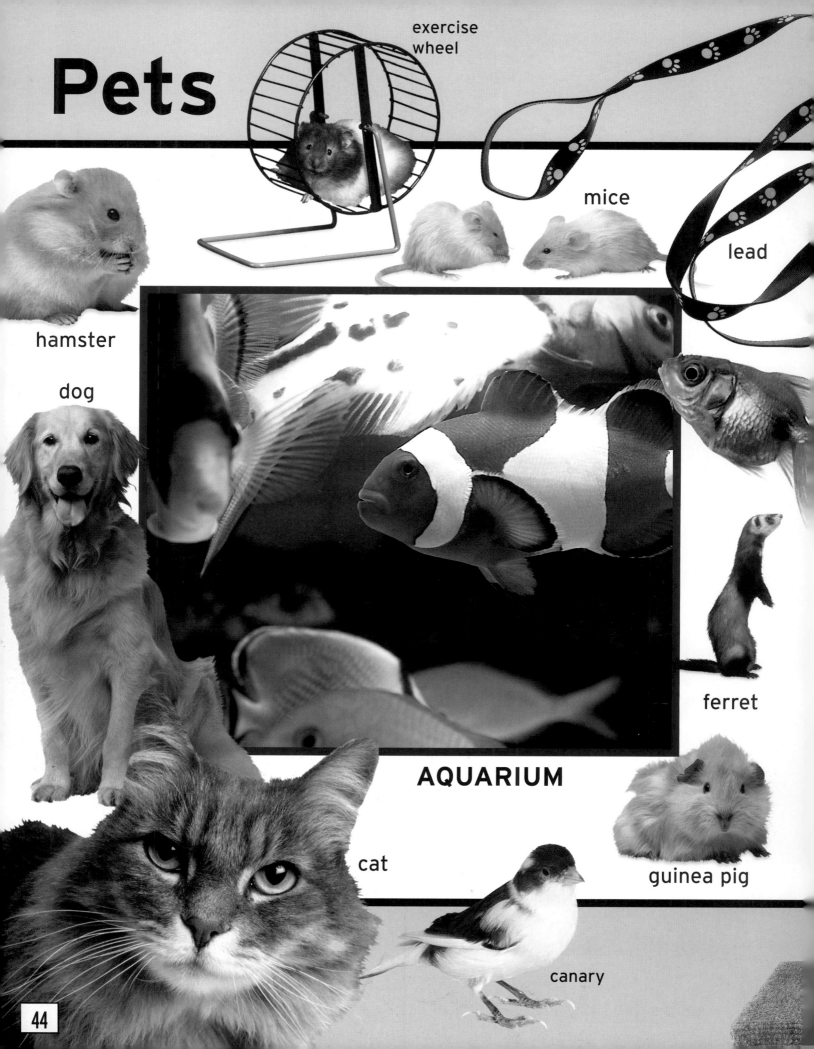

Pets

exercise wheel

mice

lead

hamster

dog

AQUARIUM

ferret

guinea pig

cat

canary

pony

kennel

collar

tug toy

rabbit

goldfish

cage

stable

scratching post

saddle

pet bed

45

A House

door knocker

mailbox

balcony

window

curtain

lawn

doormat

lock

door

wall

blind

porch

bricks

gutter

fence

garage

drive

roof

trash
can

doorknob

47

IN THE
Bedroom

chest of drawers

night-light

photo frame

toy box

trophy

alarm clock

quilt   *pillow*

BED

books

**The Folk of the
Faraway Tree**

dressing gown

wardrobe

slippers

hobby horse

mattress

pajamas

hat tree

teddy bear

rug

poster

49

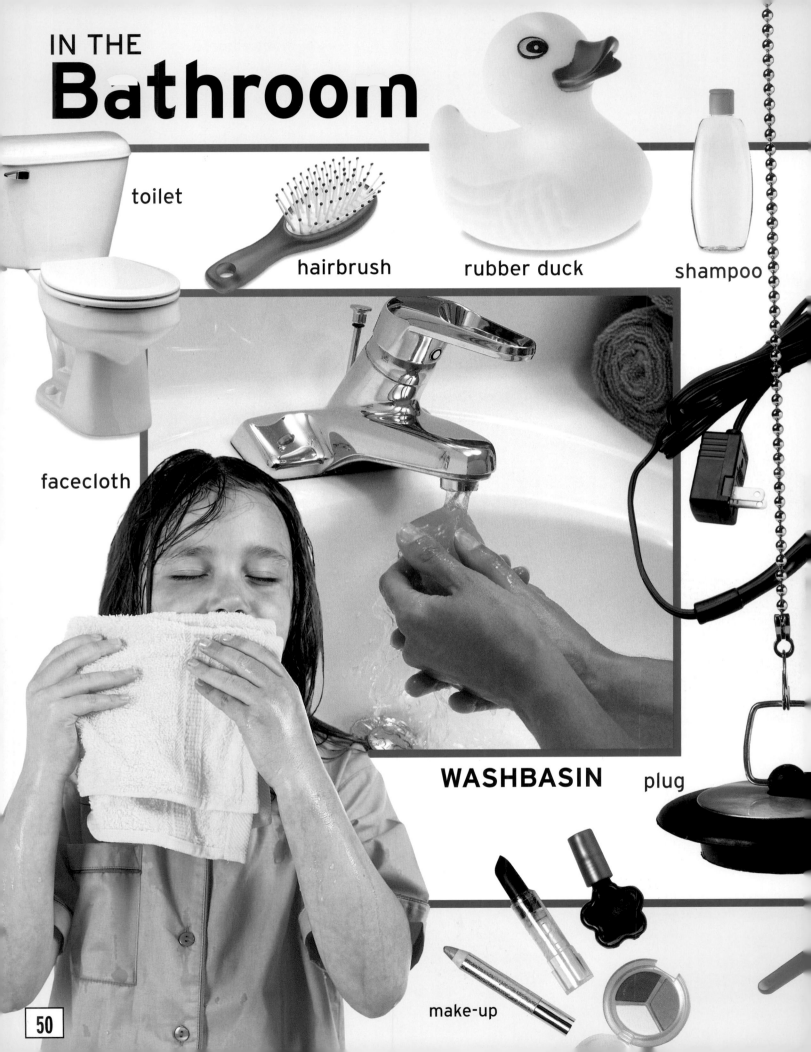

IN THE
Bathroom

toilet

hairbrush

rubber duck

shampoo

facecloth

WASHBASIN

plug

make-up

medicine

tissues

comb

toothpaste

toilet paper

hairdryer

shower

mirror

towel

bath

toothbrush

soap

bubble bath

51

IN THE
Family Room

video recorder

coffee table

lamp

remote
control

rocking
chair

cushion

BOOKSHELF

vase

television

compact disc

video cassettes

picture

carpet

beanbag

games table

coasters

headphones

sofa

newspaper

stereo

magazines

53

IN THE
Cupboard

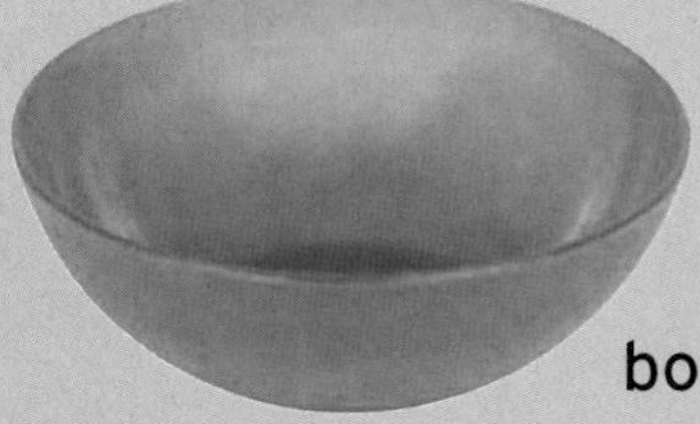

bowl

saucepan

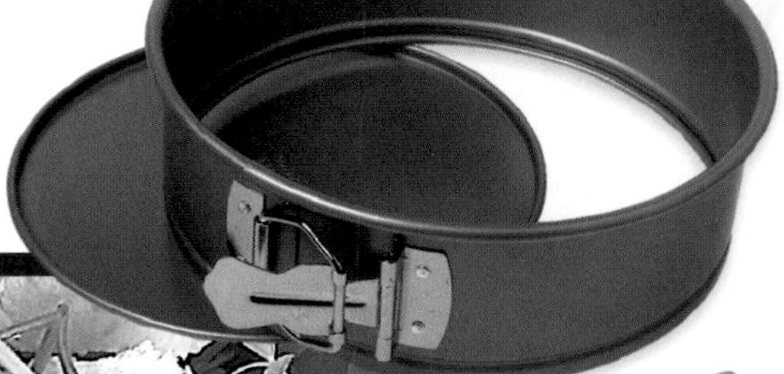

cake tin

detergent

plate

PLATTER

sponge

teapot

cup

dishtowel

rubber gloves

rolling pin

wooden spoon

glass

knife

fork

spoon

tray

egg-beater

fry pan

jug

57

envelope

desk

adhesive tape

scissors

calculator

eraser

computer disks

NOTEBOOK AND PEN

pencils

dictionary

stapler

diary

telephone

desk chair

sharpener

paper clip

computer

ruler

paper

glue

HOUSEHOLD Items

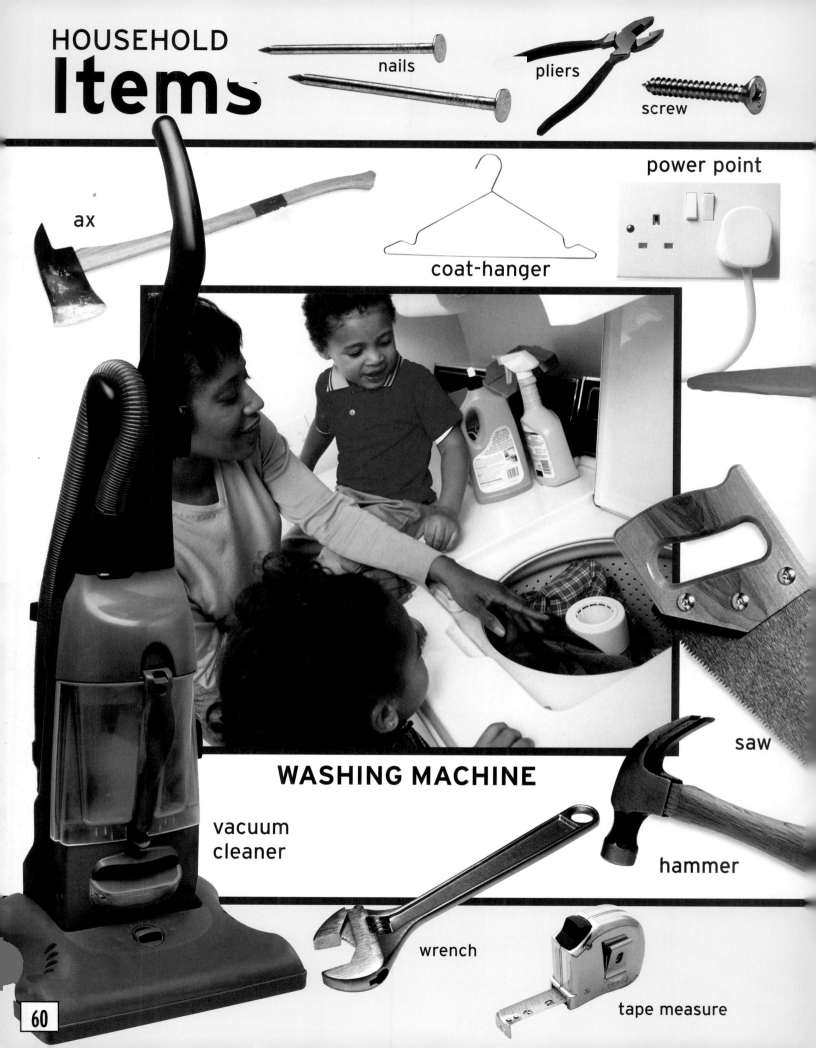

nails

pliers

screw

ax

coat-hanger

power point

WASHING MACHINE

vacuum cleaner

saw

hammer

wrench

tape measure

paintbrush

screwdrivers

iron

dryer

ladder

ironing board

tool kit

paint tin

electric drill

Birthday Party

plastic plates

candy

HAPPY

banner

birthday card

plastic cup

BIRTHDAY CAKE

wrapping paper

presents

candles

take-home bag

streamers

fruit drink

bow

party whistles

invitation

straws

badge

paper hat

birthday girl

mask

friends

party game

63

Fancy Dress

wand

bumblebee

glitter

Little Bo Peep

king

butterfly

mouse

octopus

flower

puss

tiara

fairy wings

sea lion

costume

bunny

starfish

puppy

calf

pirate

wig

clown

Toys

dice

doll's house

dinosaur

wagon

soldier

tiger

Rr Ss Tt Uu Vv Ww Xx Yy

Aa Bb Cc Dd

g Hh Ii

Ee

gg

clock

ball

key

Mm Nn Oo

Bb

Ss sciss

rose

Yy Zz

zebra

dragon

checkerboard

blackboard

PUZZLE

cowboy

cube

skipping rope

doll

cards

spaceship

robot

tricycle

blocks

slinky

dominoes

marbles

67

FAVORITE Things

kite

jewelry

boomerang

money

piggy bank

crayons

penguin

SEE-SAW

telescope

ukulele

stickers

scarf

magnet

quilt

fishing rod

chess set

coconut

Frisbee

tutu

radio

yo-yo

SPORTS
Equipment

basketball

rollerblades

baseball glove

bicycle helmet

cricket bat

dartboard

sailboard

SURFBOARD

soccer ball

flippers

baseball bat

ice skates

whistle

skis

stopwatch

darts

bicycle

goggles

wetsuit

tennis racket

football

hockey stick

MUSICAL
Instruments

bells

flute

clarinet

triangle

harp

ACOUSTIC GUITAR

cello

maracas

xylophone

accordion

piano

recorder

banjo

tambourine

trumpet

cymbals

saxophone

bagpipes

drums

electric
guitar

violin

73

ON THE
Farm

scarecrow

horse

foal

chick

hen

pig

donkey

duck

SHEEPDOG

lamb

rooster

tractor

cow

farmer

farmhouse

goat

sheep

field

goose

hay bale

gate

AT THE
Beach

ice cream

beach ball

deckchair

seaweed

sunscreen

ROCK POOL

swim ring

shells

sea

bucket
and spade

sandcastle

beach
umbrella

sand

seagull

sailboat

swimsuit

sunhat

drink

sandals

basket

sunglasses

Camping

camp bed

hiking boot

trail mix

Swiss army knife

binoculars

thermos

gas lamp

camping stove

MAP

compass

rope

matches

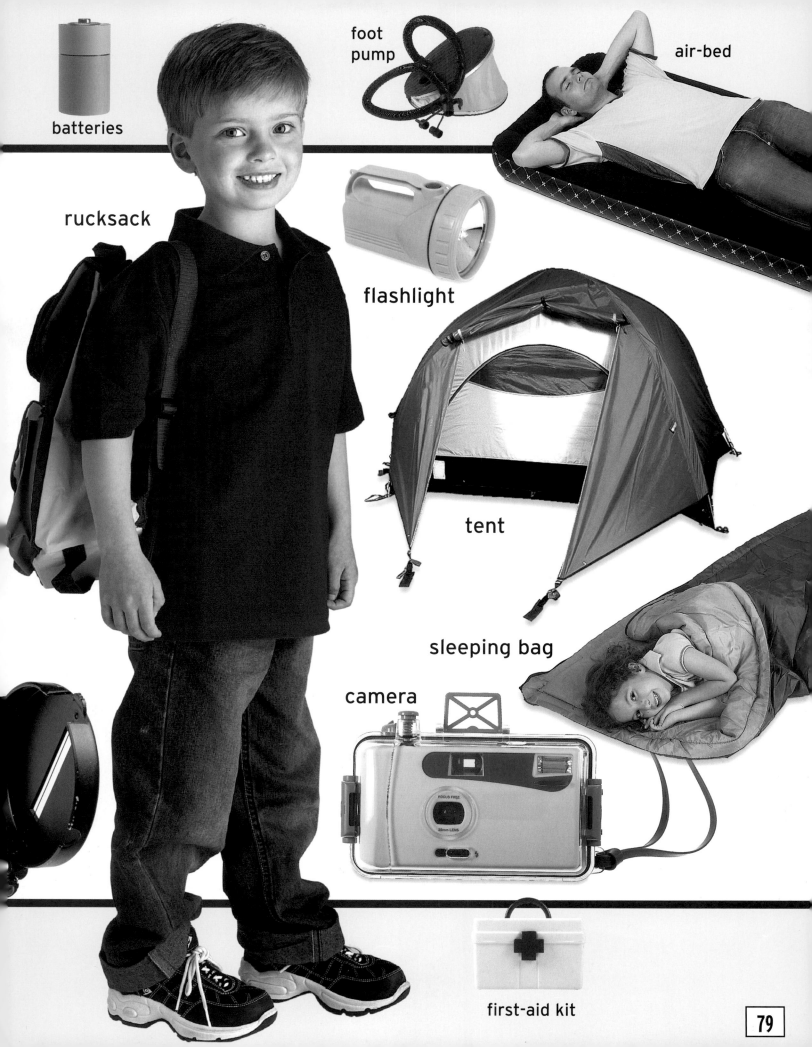

batteries

foot pump

air-bed

rucksack

flashlight

tent

sleeping bag

camera

first-aid kit

Transport

helicopter

bus

ambulance

cab

wheelchair

BOAT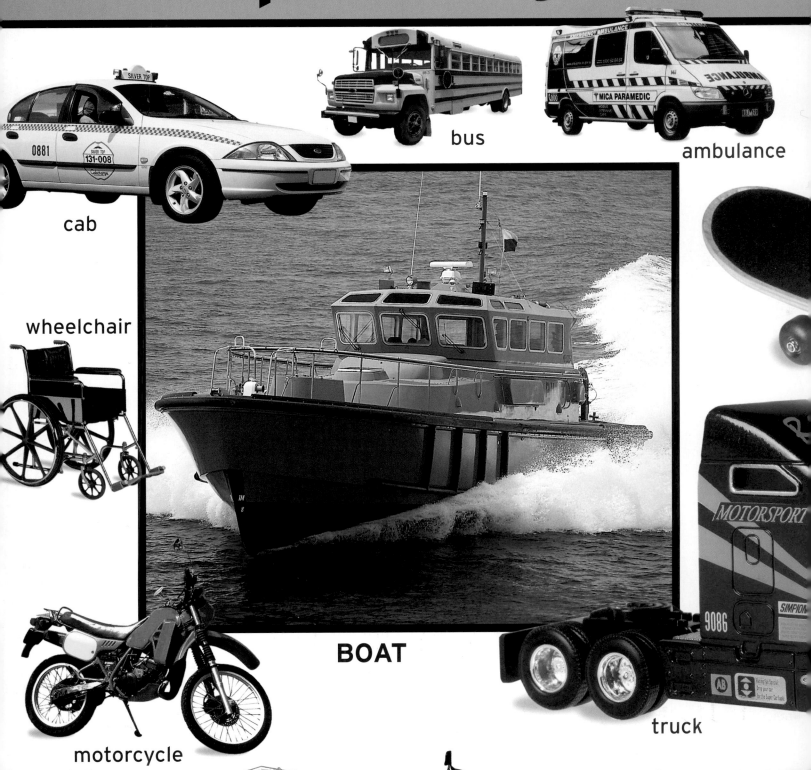

truck

motorcycle

fire engine

scooter

jet ski

car

ship

airplane

skateboard

yacht

hot-air balloon

DTM

racing car

submarine

train

PEOPLE
at Work

electrician

chef

sailor

ballerina

doctor

scientist

FIREFIGHTERS

artist

decorator

detective

82

judge

soccer player

plumber

boxer

waiter

astronaut

builder

nurse

office worker

teacher

83

Actions

walking

climbing

drawing

talking

hugging

sitting

HIDING

crying

reading

84

drinking

running

sleeping

playing

cutting

eating

kicking

jumping

frowning

reaching

writing

laughing

85

Opposites

open   closed

fat

dry

thin

wet

over

under

push

pull

down

up

young

old

short

long

empty

full

big

clean

small

dirty

Numbers

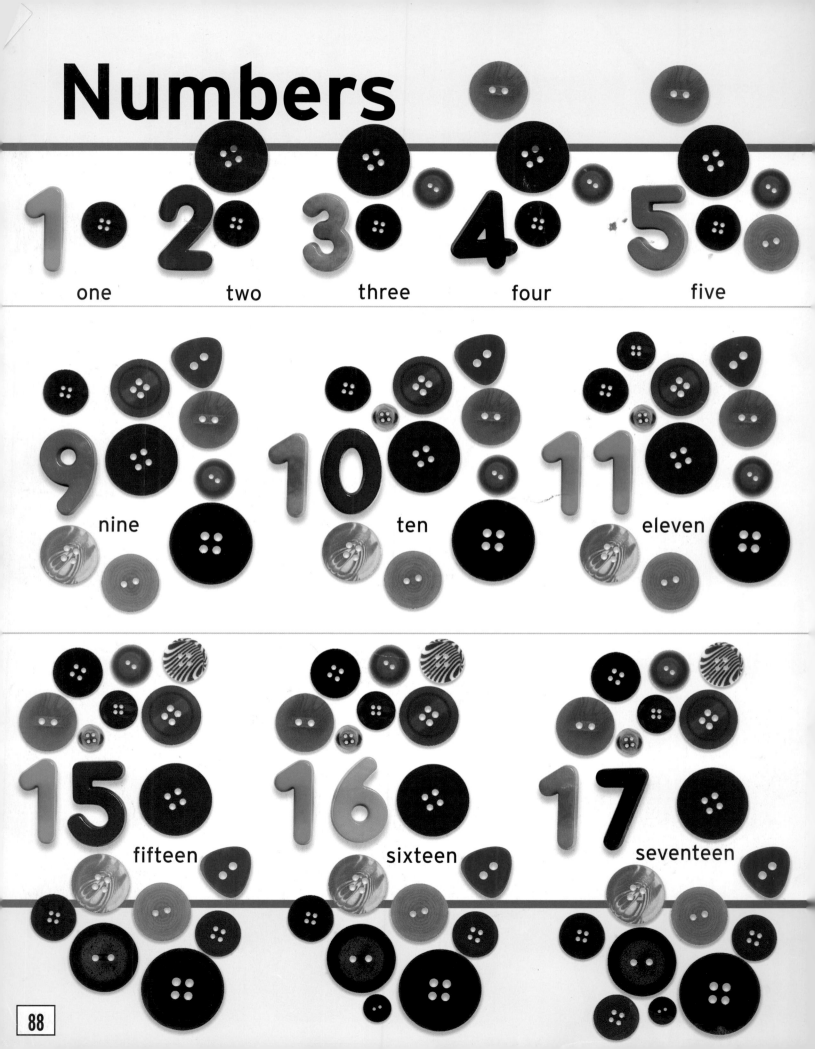

1 one
2 two
3 three
4 four
5 five

9 nine
10 ten
11 eleven

15 fifteen
16 sixteen
17 seventeen

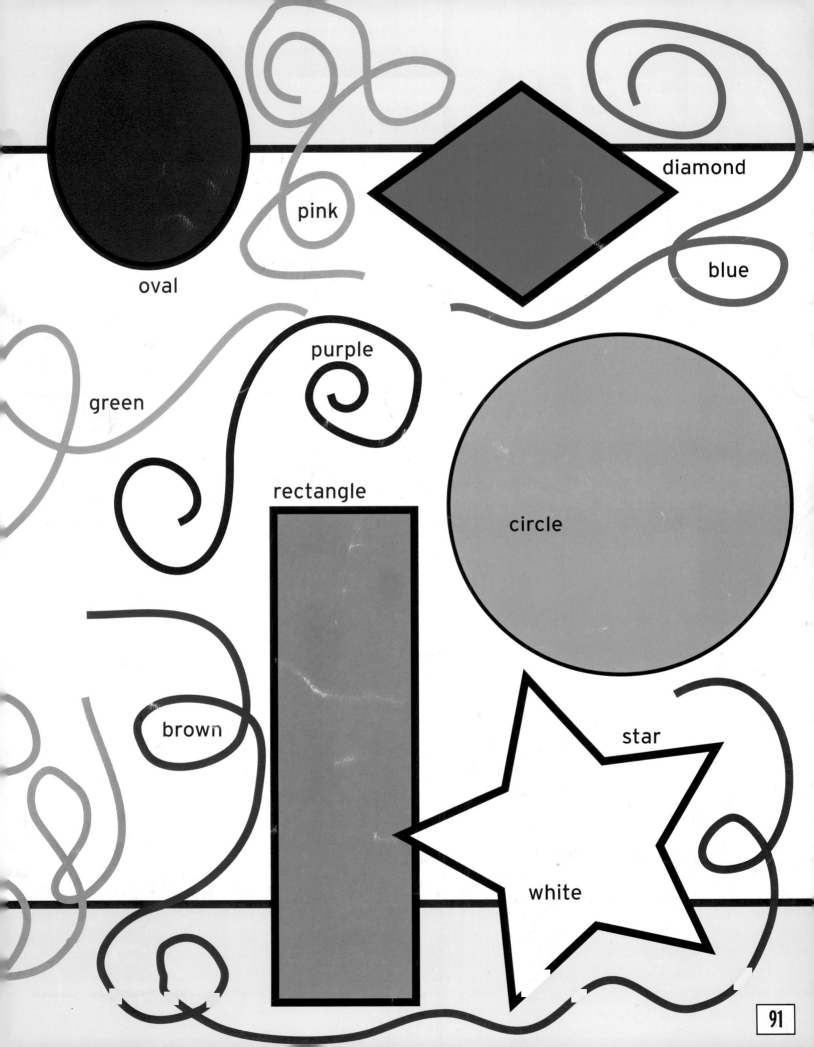

oval

pink

diamond

blue

purple

green

rectangle

circle

brown

star

white

Flags

Belgium

Mexcio

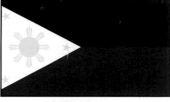

Phillipines

Australia

Singapore

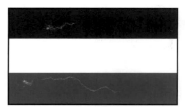

Hungary

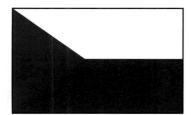

The Czech
Republic

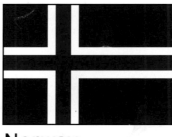

Norway

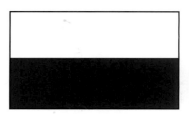

Poland

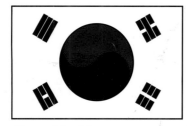

South Korea

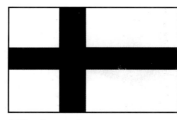

Finland

United Kingdom

Egypt

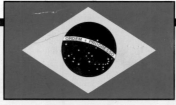

Brazil

South Africa

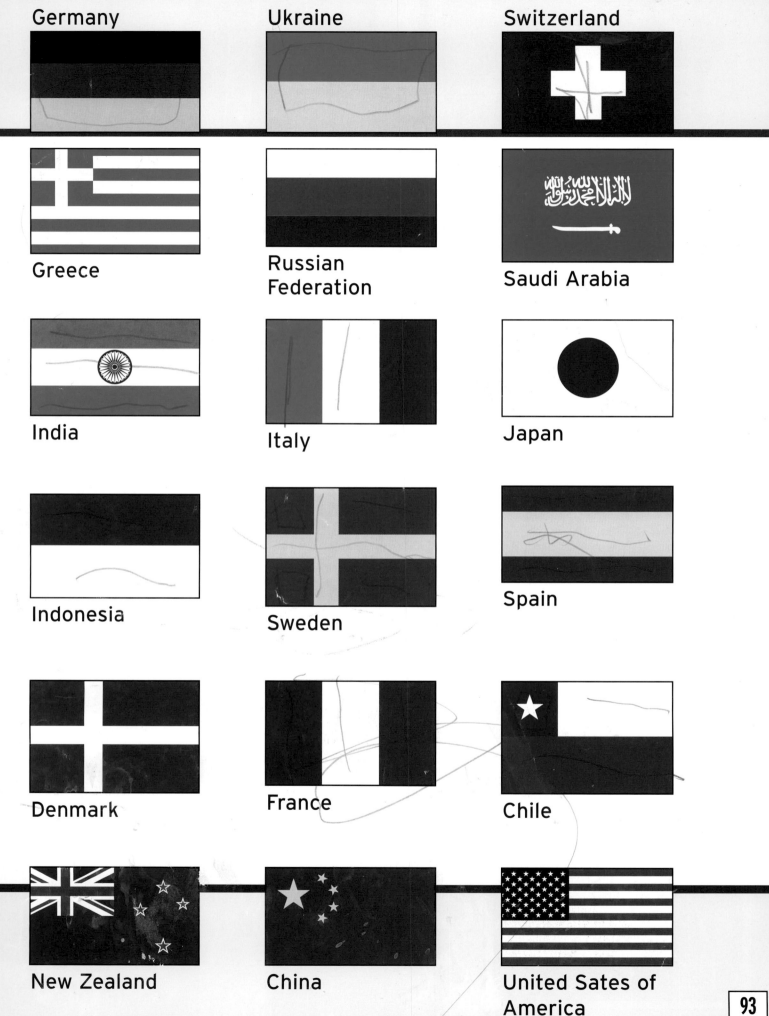

Germany

Ukraine

Switzerland

Greece

Russian Federation

Saudi Arabia

India

Italy

Japan

Indonesia

Sweden

Spain

Denmark

France

Chile

New Zealand

China

United Sates of America

93

THE Earth and Sky

clouds

Earth

wind

forest

MOUNTAIN

lightning

desert

eclipse

rain

iceberg

river

moon

pond

rainbow

stars

storm

sun

volcano

cave

waterfall

pasture